Texas
Mammals

Includes:

Texas Ecoregions

Habitats and Habits

Small Mammal Activities

Dog-like Mammal Activities

Cat-like Mammal Activities

Hoofed Mammal Activities

Bat Activities

Marine Mammals

Wildlife Identification

Wildlife Respect

Waterford Press

www.waterfordpress.com

Introduction

All North American mammals give birth to live young, which feed on milk from their mother's mammary glands. Because there are so many different habitats in Texas, it is home to over 142 different species of mammals. Some are very rare, and some are only found in Texas. From dog-like mammals like coyotes, to bats, to hoofed mammals like pronghorns, to the extremely fascinating armadillo, there is an abundance of fascinating wildlife to appreciate in Texas.

Texas Ecoregions

Ecoregions are areas that share the same climate, geology, soils, wildlife and land formations. There are 10 different ecoregions in Texas.

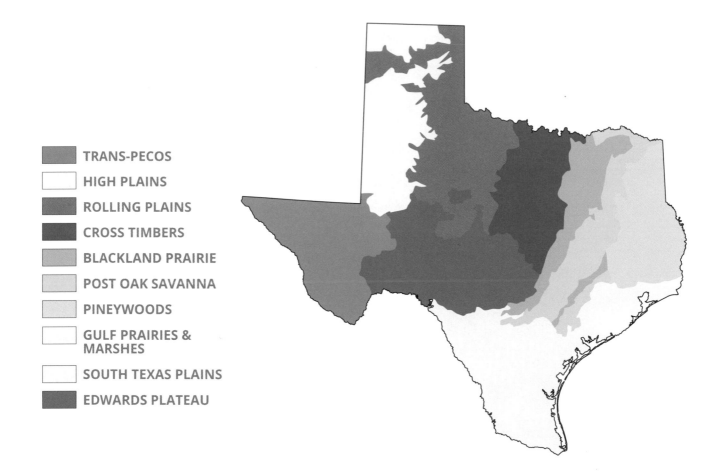

TRANS-PECOS

HIGH PLAINS

ROLLING PLAINS

CROSS TIMBERS

BLACKLAND PRAIRIE

POST OAK SAVANNA

PINEYWOODS

GULF PRAIRIES & MARSHES

SOUTH TEXAS PLAINS

EDWARDS PLATEAU

Texas Ecoregions

Trans-Pecos
From desert valleys and plains to wooded mountains,
the Trans-Pecos region extends from the far west
part of Texas to the Pecos River.

High Plains
The High Plains is a fairly level plateau. The
Caprock Escarpment separates it from the Rolling Plains.

Rolling Plains
The Rolling Plains is where many rivers and
tributaries in Texas begin.

Cross Timbers
The Cross Timbers area has a lot of trees as well as irregular
prairies and plains. It is found in north and central Texas.

Blackland Prairie
This region gets its name from the fertile,
black soils for which it is known.

Post Oak Savanna
There are many plants and animals here with ranges that extend
as far east as the forests and as far north as the Great Plains.

Pineywoods
The Pineywoods in East Texas are home to forests of tall
hardwoods and rolling hills covered with oaks and pines.

Gulf Prairies & Marshes
Streams and rivers divide this nearly level plain as
they flow into the Gulf of Mexico.

South Texas Plains
This region is known for its subtropical woodlands and
patches of palms, as well as thorny shrubs and trees.

Edwards Plateau
Known for spring-fed rivers and stony hills, Edwards Plateau is
part of an area sometimes called Texas Hill Country.

Find My Home

A habitat provides everything an animal needs for survival: food, shelter, water, the right temperature and protection from predators (animals who prey on other living things). Bears are large animals that need big caves or dens. Beavers use wood to build lodges in the middle of ponds. Squirrels build their nests high up in tree branches. Mice often build tiny woven nests in the branches of bushy shrubs.

Draw a line between the animal and its home.

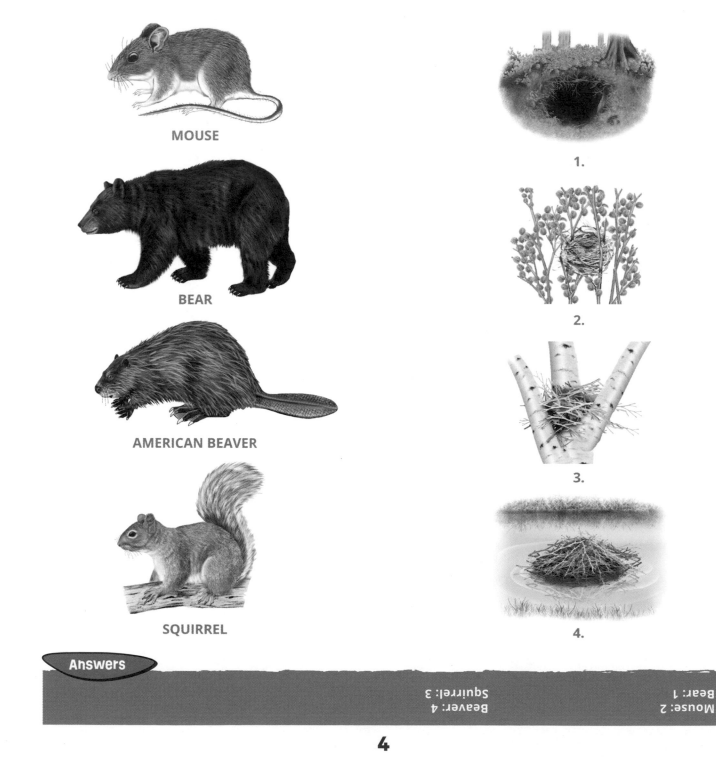

MOUSE

BEAR

AMERICAN BEAVER

SQUIRREL

1.

2.

3.

4.

Food Chain

A food chain is the order in which animals feed on other plants or animals.

Producers – A producer takes the sun's energy and stores it as food.

Consumers – A consumer feeds on other living things to get energy. Consumers can include herbivores, carnivores and omnivores.

Decomposers – A decomposer consumes waste and dead organisms for energy.

Label each living organism below as a producer, consumer or decomposer.

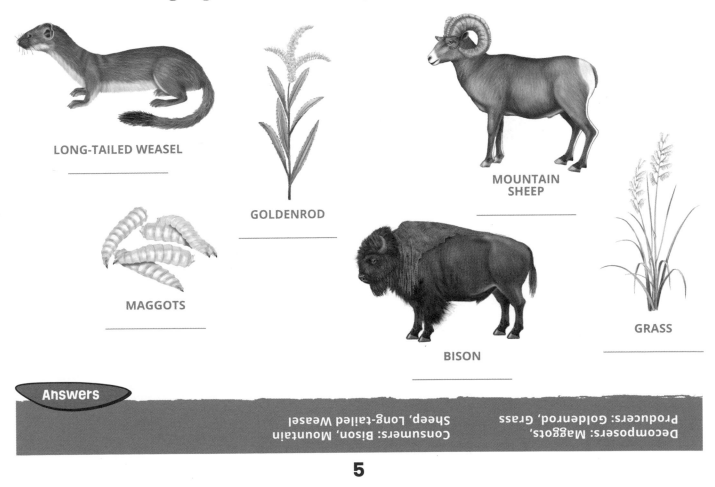

LONG-TAILED WEASEL
_____

GOLDENROD
_____

MAGGOTS
_____

MOUNTAIN SHEEP
_____

BISON
_____

GRASS
_____

What Does it Eat? Tell by its Teeth

Omnivores – eat both plants and animals. Their different types of teeth are a result of their diverse diet, which includes many different types of food. Their teeth include incisors (cutting teeth), canines (stabbing teeth) and molars (grinding teeth).

Herbivores – eat primarily plants, including grasses, shrubs, leaves and nuts. They usually have large front incisors (used to snap off plant stems and twigs) and prominent flat molars for grinding their food into tiny bits.

Carnivores – eat primarily meat. Carnivorous mammals have large canines for tearing meat apart and sharp molars for breaking it into chunks. Most cats have molars adapted for slicing rather than grinding meat.

Draw a line between the animal and its teeth.

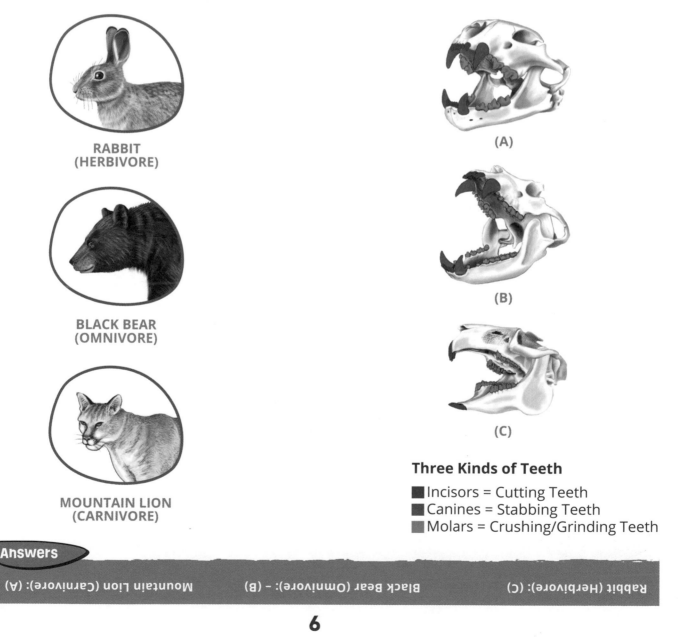

RABBIT (HERBIVORE)

BLACK BEAR (OMNIVORE)

MOUNTAIN LION (CARNIVORE)

(A)

(B)

(C)

Three Kinds of Teeth

■ Incisors = Cutting Teeth
■ Canines = Stabbing Teeth
■ Molars = Crushing/Grinding Teeth

You are What you Eat

Draw a line between the animal and its diet.

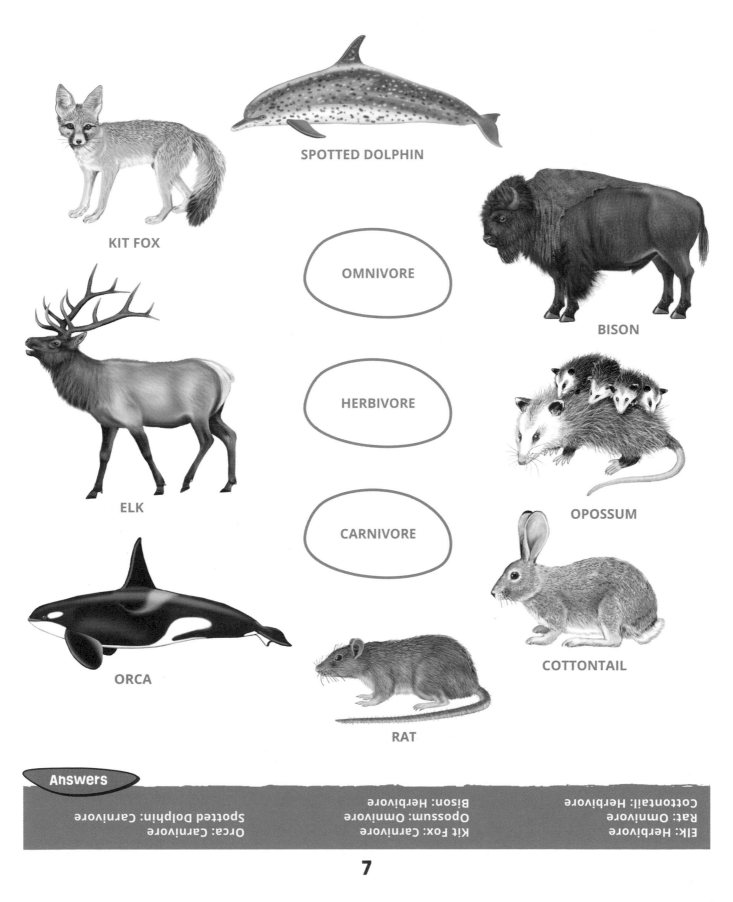

SPOTTED DOLPHIN

KIT FOX

OMNIVORE

BISON

HERBIVORE

ELK

OPOSSUM

CARNIVORE

ORCA

COTTONTAIL

RAT

Predator or Prey?

By looking at the location of the eyes on an animal's head, you can tell whether it is a predator (hunter) or prey (hunted).

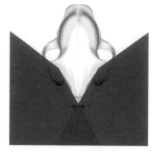

■ = Field of vision

Remember, "Eyes in front, likes to hunt; eyes at side, likes to hide."

Animals with eyes that face forward (like most carnivores) have a better ability to see depth, which makes it easier for them to move and hunt.

Animals with eyes on the side of their head (like most herbivores) have a better ability see on either side of them, which allows them to identify predators approaching from the side.

Draw a line. Which animals are predators or prey?

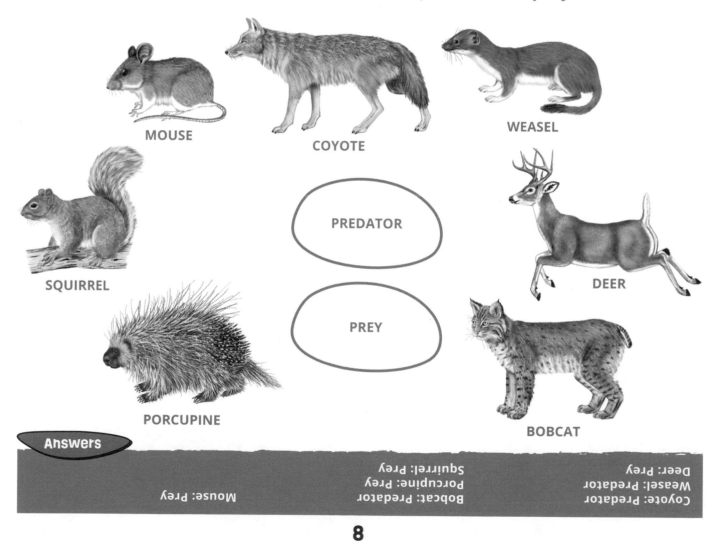

MOUSE

COYOTE

WEASEL

SQUIRREL

PREDATOR

DEER

PORCUPINE

PREY

BOBCAT

Word Search

Small mammals occupy nearly every ecosystem on the planet and fill a very important role. An ecosystem is a community of living organisms that interact with each other and their environment. Many small mammals are secondary consumers and have a beneficial impact on plant communities, but they are also the primary food source for many different predators. Because the many different types of habitats allow for a wide assortment of animals to thrive, the small mammals of Texas range broadly from the Kangaroo Rat, found only in Texas, to the very common House Mouse.

Find these common small mammals in the puzzle.

SKUNK

MUSKRAT

GRAY SQUIRREL

GROUND SQUIRREL

```
M L I A T G N I R U O T U E
U S S Q M I N T R O O S O D
I K O I H O U S E M O U S E
L I A T N O T T O C I M S R
L E R R I U Q S D N U O R G
C T L E R R I U Q S Y A R G
U U K R I O U R K A C I I A
N O R T N R A R I R N R Q E
R U R S K S A N A I M E N N
N R M I N T S L A K R S M S
U L O I U I I L L R U S I
Y O O L K Q O L I O C E E U
R Q O T S R O R R C N G R I
O O R O N S C R A C C O O N
```

Answers

RACCOON

HOUSE MOUSE

COTTONTAIL

RINGTAIL

Make Words

The **Nine-banded Armadillo** is the official state small mammal of Texas. It is a cat-sized, insect-eating mammal with a bony, scaled shell that protects it from predators. A skilled digger, it is known for digging up insects and other invertebrates (organisms without backbones, like worms). Its diet consists mostly of grubs, but it will sometimes eat berries or bird eggs. Adaptable, it can be found living in brush, woods, scrub and grasslands across Texas, everywhere except the Trans-Pecos ecoregion.

How many words can you make from the letters in Armadillo?

_____   _____

_____   _____

_____   _____

_____   _____

_____   _____

_____   _____

_____   _____

_____   _____

Maze

Moles are mammals that live underground in tunnels and feed on plant roots and small animals. When tunneling, the mole pushes up small mounds of dirt above the ground.

Help this mole find its way through the tunnel.

ENTER

Origami

Starting with a square piece of paper, follow the folding instructions below to create a squirrel.

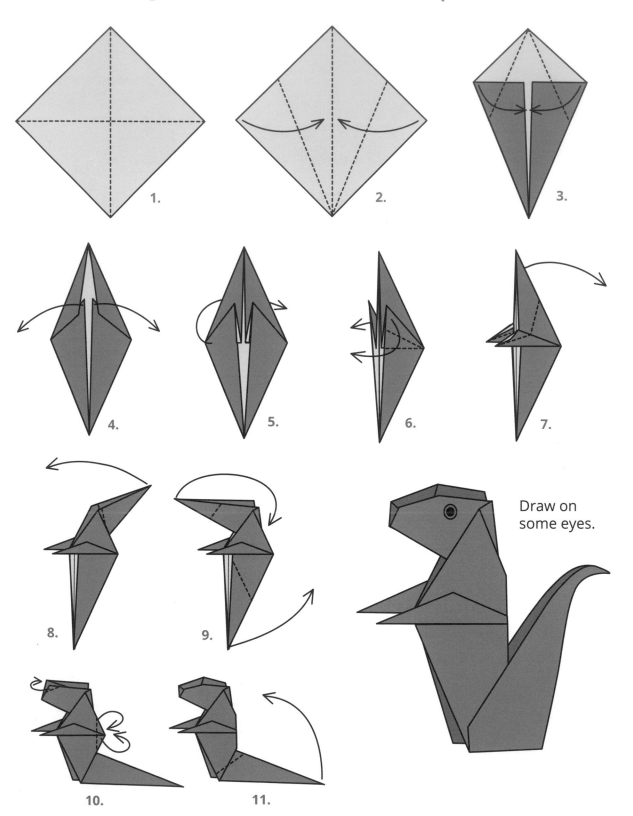

1.

2.

3.

4.

5.

6.

7.

8.

9.

Draw on some eyes.

10.

11.

Be an Artist

Draw this Kangaroo Rat by copying one square at a time.

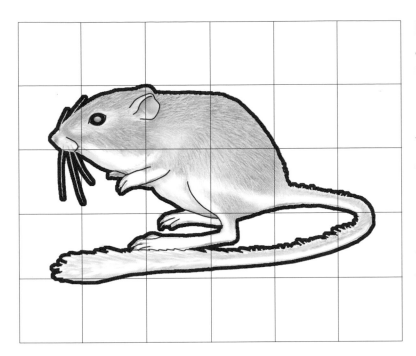

Kangaroo Rats

are neither kangaroos nor rats. Unique to Texas, the Texas Kangaroo Rat is more closely related to pocket mice and gophers. This large, four-toed critter has very strong hind legs and long, furry tails. With a body only 4 in. (10cm) long, it can jump an astounding 8 ft. (2.4 m). That's the equivalent of a human jumping 144 ft. (44 m)! These animals are rare and thought to be at risk of becoming endangered. Endangered animals are in danger of becoming extinct.

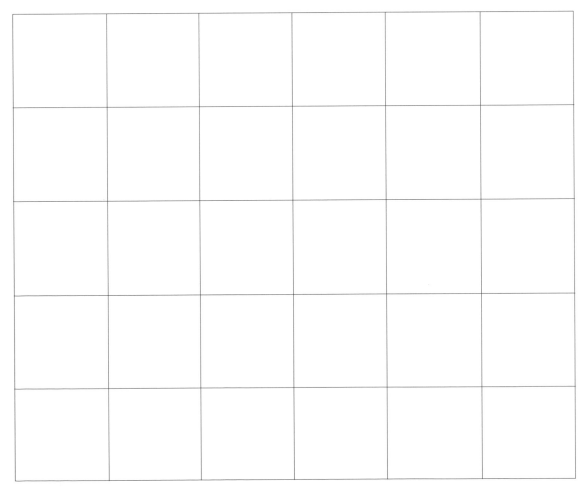

Make Words

The **Porcupine** – This prickly rodent may have as many as 30,000 barbed quills near its rear end, which it uses in self-defense. Contrary to popular legend, a porcupine cannot shoot its quills; instead, it shows its barbed tail and rear end and lashes out at a human or animal that makes it feel threatened. The quills come out when the tail hits something. The porcupine is an herbivore and eats vegetation like leaves, twigs, bark and flowers. It is mostly nocturnal (active at night) but will sometimes look for food during the day. It is an excellent climber and is usually seen in trees.

How many words can you make from the letters in its name?

Answers

Possible answers include: coin, con, cop, cone, cope, core, corn, crop, cup, cure, icon, in, incur, nice, nip, nope, opine, or, pin, pine, pip, pipe, pop, pope, pour, pup, pure, rice, ripe, rope, ruin, up, urine, urn

Origami

Start with a square piece of paper and follow the simple
folding instructions below to create a rabbit.

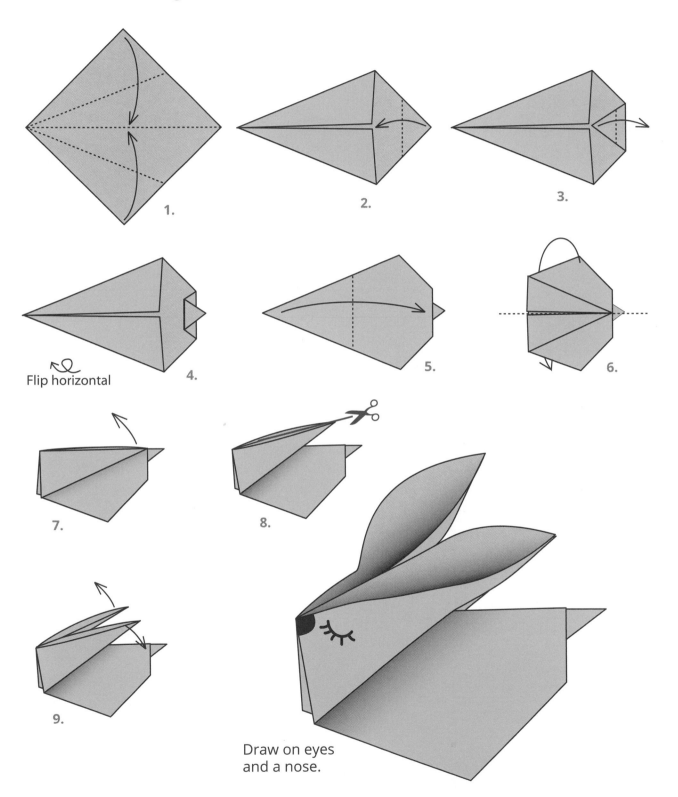

Flip horizontal

1.

2.

3.

4.

5.

6.

7.

8.

9.

Draw on eyes
and a nose.

Shadow Know-How

Now that you have learned about many common small mammals in Texas, **can you identify these animals from their shadows?**

Word Scramble

These small members of the Canidae family (dog-like mammals) use their intelligence and ability to move quickly to survive, rather than size or strength. They are very adaptable animals and can be found in all parts of Texas. The four species of fox in Texas all have special characteristics that allow them to thrive in very different habitats.

Unscramble the letters to form the names of these foxes.

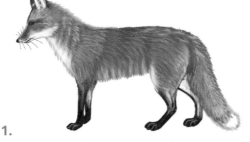

1.
The largest fox in Texas, it can reach up to 30 pounds and is usually red to orange-colored with dark feet and white on the tip of the tail and underbelly. It is found in forests, meadows and farms in the eastern and north-central parts of the state.

EDRXFO

2.
The only member of the Canidae family who can climb trees, it is usually seen with combinations of red, gray, white, brown and black fur with black on the tip of its tail.

OMCOMNYARGFXO

3.
This pale fox is only found in the Trans-Pecos region of Texas because it prefers arid (very dry) habitats with loose soil to build its den. It has large, round ears that sit high on its head.

IKTOXF

4.
This small fox averages only 4-5 pounds in weight. The size of a house cat, it lives in the panhandle region of Texas and builds dens in open fields, farms, prairies and deserts. It is a fast fox (swift, like its name) and can run up to 30 mph (48.3 kph).

WSITFOFX

Answers

Be an Artist

Draw this coyote by copying one square at a time.

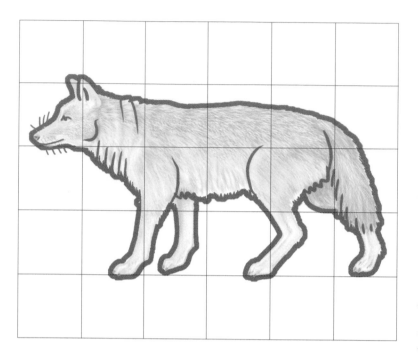

The **Coyote** was a native inhabitant of Texas but now has adapted to thrive almost everywhere in the United States. "Adapted" means the animal has developed a body part or behavior that helps it survive better in its environment. Extremely intelligent, with a keen sense of smell and sight, this dog-like animal takes advantage of its opportunities and will eat almost anything. A coyote's diet is mostly made up of rabbit, rodents and insects, but it will eat lizards, snakes, fruit, vegetables, fish or even carrion (dead animals). Unlike wolves, dogs or foxes, the coyote runs with its tail down instead of sticking straight out or up.

Who am I?

From the 3-foot ocelot roaming the native brush of South Texas to the very large mountain lion making its home in cliff crevices and ledges, Texas is home to 5 species of cat, including some that are rare or endangered. These carnivores are considered keystone species for their habitats because they keep populations low by eating large herbivores (like deer) and other animals that can wipe out vegetation growth. All have short faces, keen vision, powerful bodies and retractable claws. These skilled hunters mostly stalk their prey at night and spend their days under dense cover.

Read the clues to identify these cat-like mammals.

1. I am an unspotted cat and can grow as big as 8.5 feet (2.6 meters) tall.

_____

2. I am a medium-sized cat named for my short tail.

_____

3. My beautiful spots and stripes are unique. No two of my species have the same markings.

_____

4. I am considered rare and can jump very high for my small size.

_____

5. I am the third largest cat in the world, have either black fur or spots and am endangered.

_____

Antlers & Horns

Many deer, goat and sheep species will grow horns or antlers. The difference between antlers and horns is that antlers fall off and regrow every year, while horns are permanent. Males in many species use their antlers or horns to establish territory, fight for mates or defend themselves.

Draw a line between the animal and its antlers.

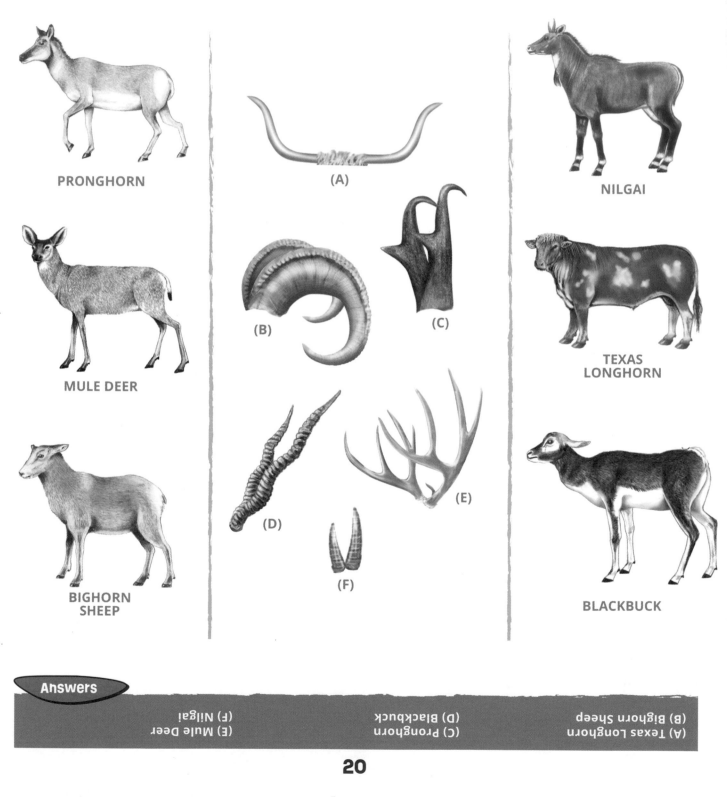

PRONGHORN

(A)

NILGAI

MULE DEER

(B)

(C)

TEXAS LONGHORN

BIGHORN SHEEP

(D)

(E)

(F)

BLACKBUCK

Shadow Know-How

Can you identify these horned mammals?

Be an Artist

Draw this Wild Hog by copying one square at a time.

The **Wild Hog** is one of the worst invasive species in Texas. An invasive species is a living thing that was introduced to a new place where it didn't belong and can cause harm to the environment. Introduced by ranchers and sportsmen in the 1930s, it is a descendant of escaped domestic hogs or European wild hogs. It destroys large tracts of land by uprooting vegetation and causing excessive erosion. It also devours many native animals, including endangered species. It is usually black with a long grizzled coat and tusks that grow up to 9 in. (23 cm) long.

Word Search

Though they can fly like birds, bats are mammals. They hunt small prey and are rarely harmful to humans. Very beneficial native animals, they eat insects, feed on nectar and are important pollinators (an animal that helps plants grow and produce seeds by moving pollen between plants). They serve as food for predators like owls, hawks and raccoons, and their waste can be used as fertilizer. Bats like to roost in caves, tree cavities, palm fronds, buildings or under bridges. Creatures of habit, they will return year after year to the same roost.

Find these common bats in the puzzle.

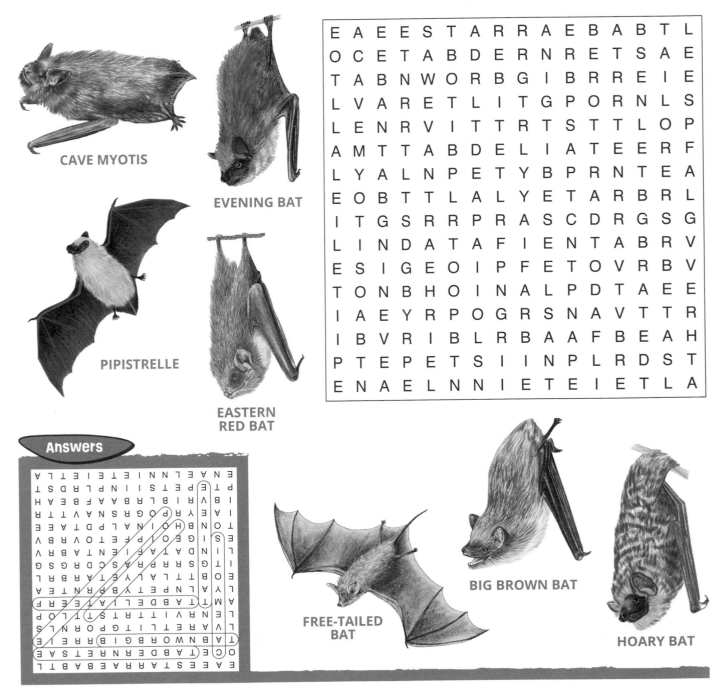

CAVE MYOTIS

EVENING BAT

PIPISTRELLE

EASTERN RED BAT

```
E A E E S T A R R A E B A B T L
O C E T A B D E R N R E T S A E
T A B N W O R B G I B R R E I E
L V A R E T L I T G P O R N L S
L E N R V I T T R T S T T L O P
A M T T A B D E L I A T E E R F
L Y A L N P E T Y B P R N T E A
E O B T T L A L Y E T A R B R L
I T G S R R P R A S C D R G S G
L I N D A T A F I E N T A B R V
E S I G E O I P F E T O V R B V
T O N B H O I N A L P D T A E E
I A E Y R P O G R S N A V T T R
I B V R I B L R B A A F B E A H
P T E P E T S I I N P L R D S T
E N A E L N N I E T E I E T L A
```

Answers

FREE-TAILED BAT

BIG BROWN BAT

HOARY BAT

23

Connect the Dots

Connect the dots to reveal this flying mammal that uses radar-like echolocation to find its way in the dark.

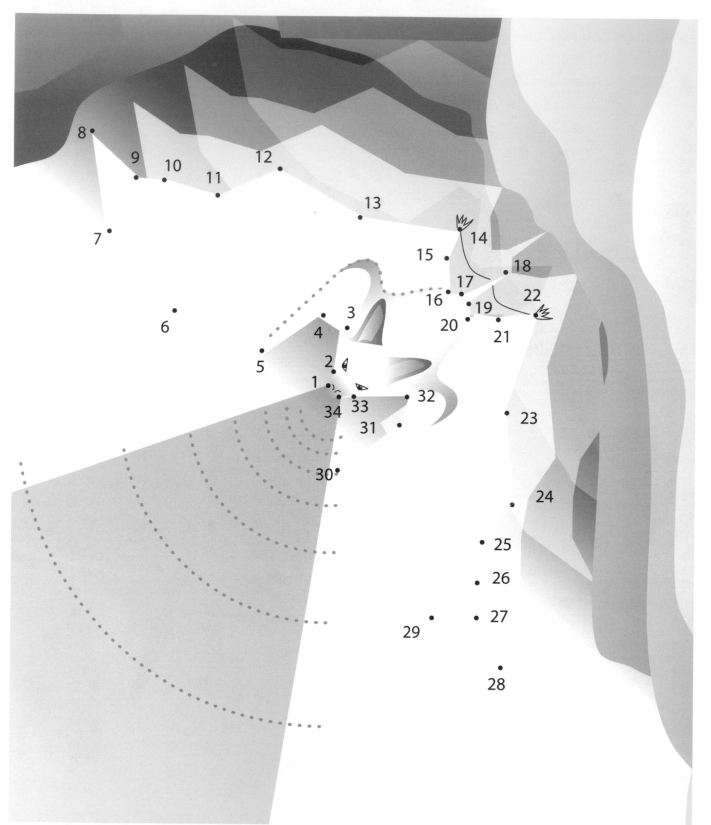

Word Search

Dolphins and whales may look like fish, but they are very different in many ways. Fish have vertical (running up and down) tail flukes, while dolphins and whales have horizontal (in a straight line) ones. Fish use gills to get oxygen from the water while whales and dolphins breathe air from the surface using the blowholes on their heads.

Find these common marine mammals in the puzzle.

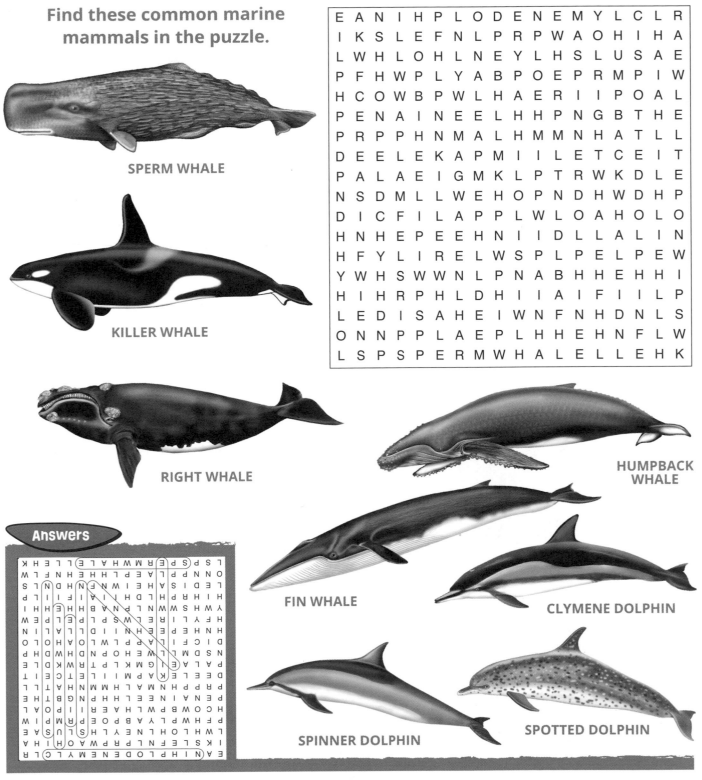

SPERM WHALE

KILLER WHALE

RIGHT WHALE

HUMPBACK WHALE

FIN WHALE

CLYMENE DOLPHIN

SPINNER DOLPHIN

SPOTTED DOLPHIN

```
E A N I H P L O D E N E M Y L C L R
I K S L E F N L P R P W A O H I H A
L W H L O H L N E Y L H S L U S A E
P F H W P L Y A B P O E P R M P I W
H C O W B P W L H A E R I I P O A L
P E N A I N E E L H H P N G B T H E
P R P P H N M A L H M M N H A T L L
D E E L E K A P M I I L E T C E I T
P A L A E I G M K L P T R W K D L E
N S D M L L W E H O P N D H W D H P
D I C F I L A P P L W L O A H O L O
H N H E P E E H N I I D L L A L I N
H F Y L I R E L W S P L P E L P E W
Y W H S W W N L P N A B H H E H H I
H I H R P H L D H I I A I F I I L P
L E D I S A H E I W N F N H D N L S
O N N P P L A E P L H H E H N F L W
L S P S P E R M W H A L E L L E H K
```

Answers

```
L S P S P E R M W H A L E L L E H K
O N N P P L A E P L H H E H N F L W
S L E D I S A H E I W N F N H D N L S
L L I I F I A I I H D L H P R H I H
I H H E H H B A N P L N W W S H W Y
W E P L E P L P S W L E R I L Y F H
N I L L A L L D I I N H E E P E H N H
O L O H A O L W L P P A L I F C I D
E L D K W R T P L K M G I E A L A P
P H D W H D N P O H E W L L M D S N
T I E C T E L I I M P A K E L E E D
L L T A H N M M H L A M N H P P R P
E H T B G N P H H L E E N I A N E P
L A O P I I R E A H L W P B W O C H
E A U S P M R P E O P B A Y L P W H F P
A S U L S H L Y E N L H O L H W L
A H I H O A W P R L N F E L S K I
R L C L Y M E N E D O L P H I N A E
```

25

Who am I?

Name these marine mammals.

1. I am also called orca.

_____

2. I am named for the shape of my nose.

_____

3. I am the second largest mammal in the world.

_____

4. I can be found in polar, temperate, and tropical waters worldwide.

_____

5. I can dive up to 200 feet.

_____

Make Words

The distinctive **Humpback Whale** has a knobby head and long, scalloped flippers that are easy to spot when it surfaces. It feeds during summer in polar waters and migrates in winter to tropical waters to breed and give birth, which is when it can be found in the Gulf of Mexico. It migrates up to 16,000 miles (25,000 kilometers) each year!

How many words can you make from the letters in its name?

_____ _____

_____ _____

_____ _____

_____ _____

_____ _____

_____ _____

_____ _____

_____ _____

Name Match

Draw a line between the marine mammal and its name.

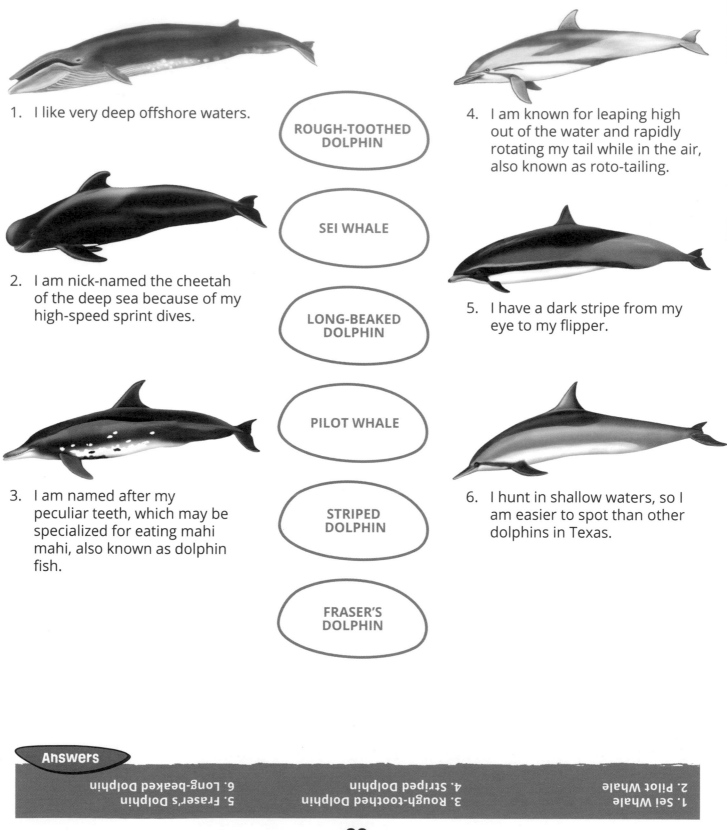

1. I like very deep offshore waters.

ROUGH-TOOTHED DOLPHIN

4. I am known for leaping high out of the water and rapidly rotating my tail while in the air, also known as roto-tailing.

SEI WHALE

2. I am nick-named the cheetah of the deep sea because of my high-speed sprint dives.

LONG-BEAKED DOLPHIN

5. I have a dark stripe from my eye to my flipper.

PILOT WHALE

3. I am named after my peculiar teeth, which may be specialized for eating mahi mahi, also known as dolphin fish.

STRIPED DOLPHIN

6. I hunt in shallow waters, so I am easier to spot than other dolphins in Texas.

FRASER'S DOLPHIN

Answers

1. Sei Whale
2. Pilot Whale
3. Rough-toothed Dolphin
4. Striped Dolphin
5. Fraser's Dolphin
6. Long-beaked Dolphin

Maze

North America's largest rodent, the American Beaver, is an herbivore who, like humans, will change its surroundings to suit its habitat needs. When a beaver moves into an area, it quickly goes to work building dams in order to create a year-round wetlands. Beaver dams provide very important habitats for thousands of species.

Help the beaver find its way to the sticks and twigs for its dam.

ENTER

Animal Tracks

An animal's track is defined by the shape of its feet, its weight and the way it walks, runs or hops. The size of a track usually tells you the size of the animal. Sandy or muddy soils are the best places to find clear tracks. The best time to look for tracks is following rains, fresh snowfalls or at dawn when the dew makes tracks easy to identify.

Draw a line between the animal and its tracks.

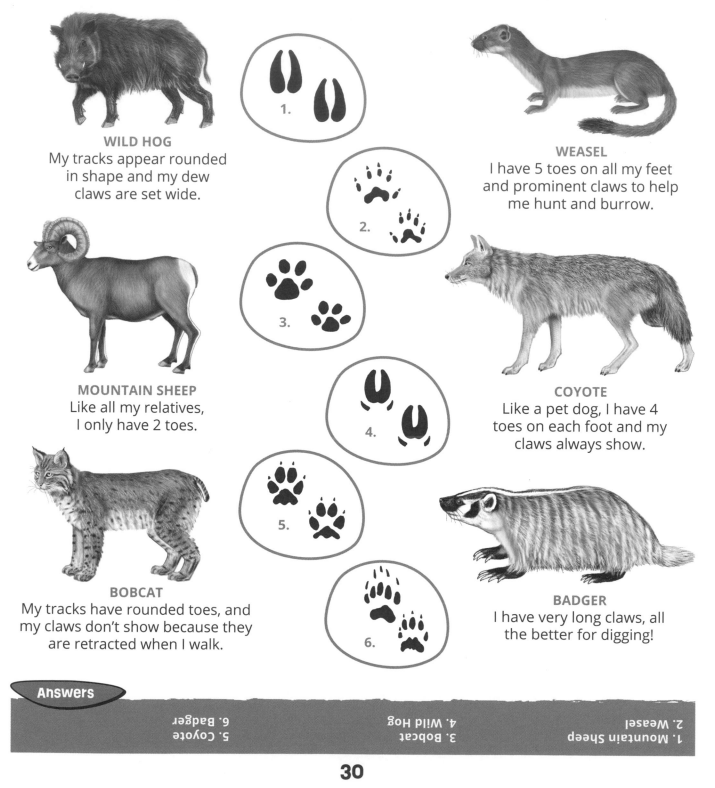

WILD HOG
My tracks appear rounded in shape and my dew claws are set wide.

MOUNTAIN SHEEP
Like all my relatives, I only have 2 toes.

BOBCAT
My tracks have rounded toes, and my claws don't show because they are retracted when I walk.

WEASEL
I have 5 toes on all my feet and prominent claws to help me hunt and burrow.

COYOTE
Like a pet dog, I have 4 toes on each foot and my claws always show.

BADGER
I have very long claws, all the better for digging!

Answers

1. Mountain Sheep
2. Weasel
3. Bobcat
4. Wild Hog
5. Coyote
6. Badger

30

Animal Tracks

Draw a line between the animal and its tracks.

MOUSE
I have light tracks with 4 toes on my front feet and 5 toes on my back feet.

OPOSSUM
I have distinctive tracks. that look like human hand prints.

JACKRABBIT
I have very long back feet and small rounded front feet.

SKUNK
My claws are often only easy to see on my front feet.

RACCOON
I have long toes and fingers, and my claw marks are always visible.

SQUIRREL
I have long back feet and short front feet.

1.
2.
3.
4.
5.
6.

Answers

Wildlife Respect

The best way to learn about wildlife is by quietly watching. Though the possibility of getting a better look—or a better photo—can be tempting, getting too close can be stressful to a wild animal. It is important to remember that humans are the visitors in wild habitats.

Here are some ways you can help reduce the number of disruptive human encounters that wild animals experience:

1. Know the site before you go.

2. When taking photos, do not use a flash, which can disturb animals.

3. Give animals room to move and act naturally.

4. Visit after breakfast and before dinner when wild animals are less active.

5. Do not touch or disturb the animals.

6. Do not feed the animals.

7. Store your food and take your trash with you.

8. Read and respect signs.

9. Do not make quick movements or loud noises.

10. Report any encounters with dangerous animals.